A Cherub That Sees Them

Cover Painting: To Bed at Noon
oil on canvas 1994 by Christopher Twigg

Layout by: Bong Sto. Domingo & Adam Schmitt
Edited by Jennifer Hawes

Manufactured in Washington State by Gorham Printing

First Printing
ISBN 0-9716464-4-9

Library Of Congress
catalog card number applied for

Published by Zenane Independent Media
PO Box 47382 Seattle, WA, 98146-7382
http://www.zenane.com

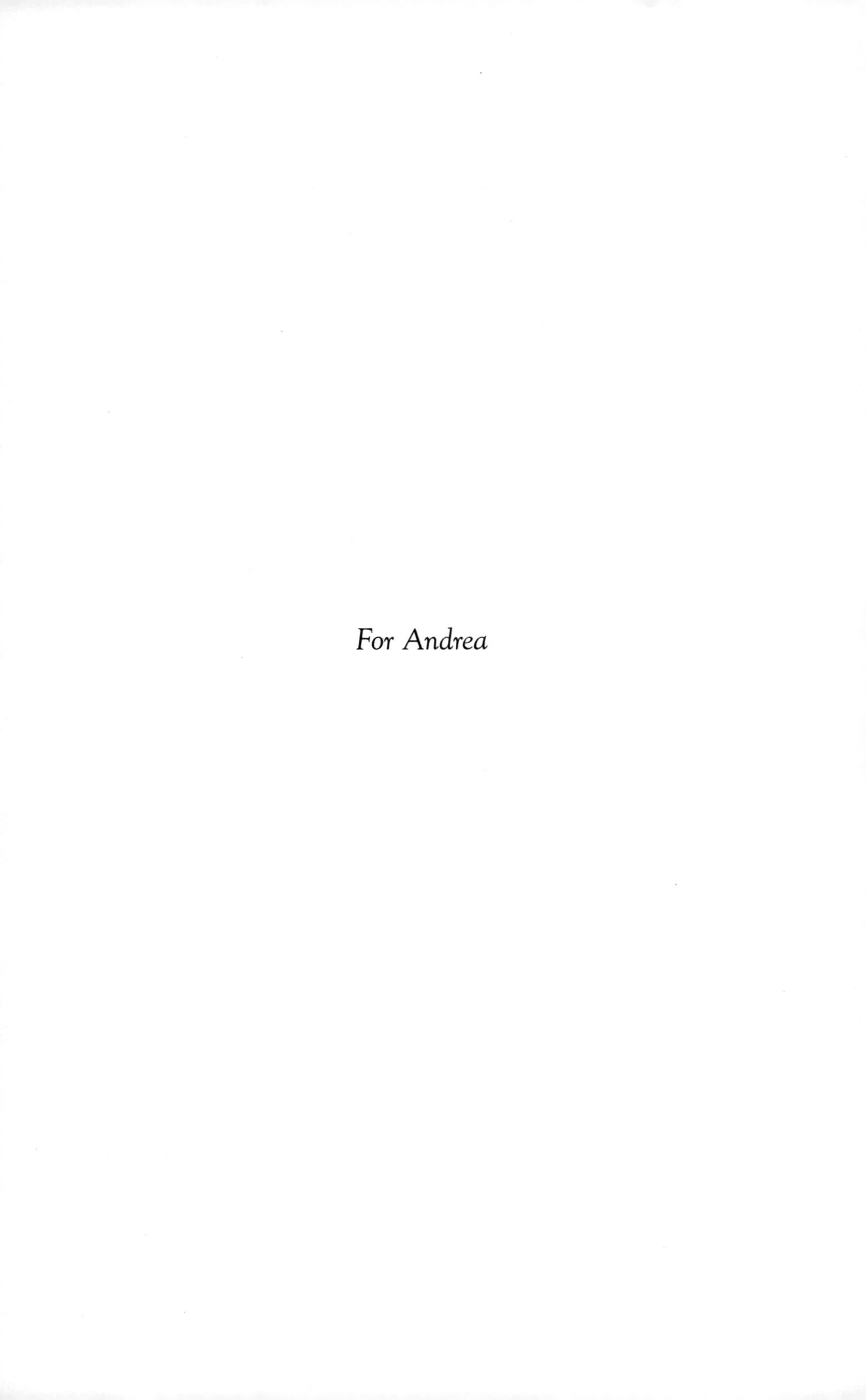

For Andrea

A Cherub That Sees Them

Christopher Twigg

ZIM

Contents

The Potato Masher

They say I mashed potatoes well last night-
my luck was with me and I got it right
I pressed the masher hard on grainy paste
and added salt and butter sweet to taste
I shook on pepper poured in milk as well
We had been worried - earlier - a smell
of burning rubber under saucepan's heat
Potatoes mashed with care were good to eat-
The openings in the masher let it through
potato leapt as potato knows how to do
and almost chip like almost like spaghetti
a finest purée - fishes in a net we
brought to our Master in the morning light
we, who had caught nothing the previous night.

To my Feet

My dear and holy feet five feet away
with shadowed valleys dark between the toes;
you love to walk over the rich spring grass,
or wet sea sand....
I call you 'the warm outposts
of my loving Self at rest'.

When I was in hospital
a lady photographer came
and photographed my feet.
Maybe they've saved lives!
by helping doctors
identify the rash
of meningitis.

Big toes move in shoes
like molluscs.
Nails tender as moons
arch under leather.

When I lost my faith
my feet never doubted;
they kept up a groundswell
of firm belief.
When I cursed God and Nature
and wanted to die
my feet were sorry as tree trunks
when the birds go hungry.

Compassionate extremities!
Lovers of carpet and meadow!
Breaking the crust of snow and sinking in!
Delighting in the sand's resilience!
Heels scuffing circles; toes
stubbed painfully on driftwood.

(You, concrete pavements, when will you respond,
draw back, or even recognize my feet?)
Oh let me not ignore their happiness,
their life of present moments, felt and lived!
How can I but repay their teaching than
with walks through sea, with walks on sand or grass?

Nicanor Parra

After his reading in Concepción
when crowds were thronging round him in the foyer
I waited patiently and took my chance.
"You come most carefully upon your hour"
said Nicanor in gentle English tones
and then "Why don't you come and visit me
in Las Cruces?", he wrote his number down
on a scrap of paper which I still treasure.
I travelled to Temuco and from there
down to the coast, stayed in an old hotel,
with rattling windows and a wild sea.
I walked along the shore and turned inland
to Indian villages, men on horseback
stopped me for cigarettes, another man
was mourning for his mother who had died.
I flew to Santiago in the night.
The next day took the bus to Las Cruces
and found a room in the Hotel Trouville.
It had a kitchen with delightful views
over the beach where bathers formed a pier.
The sea was red with seaweed, thick as soup.

They showed me where he lived behind the beach
a wooden house with gardens at the front.
His maid opened the door. "Don Christopher."
She led me through to a small study where
I sat until Don Nicanor appeared
in white like Nehru, loosely flowing white.
I nervously shook hands. My neck was stiff,
my head ached too as if I'd grapes of lead
behind the eyes. What could we talk about?
And was I an impostor in that house?
He gently gave me confidence to speak.
I asked if he thought Whitman had a sense
of humour. "*Parece que no*" he replied,
"It seems that he did not." It made him smile.
He told me how he'd rescued Robert Lowell
from drowning off the coast of Venezuela.
I said "Don Nicanor please tell me if

I'm tiring you." (For he was eighty-six).
"I'm skilled at getting rid of people who
are wearying. You'll know when I get tired."
We drank our tea and then he opened wine
and after supper pointed out the lights
of San Antonio beyond the bay,
the *lindo puerto*, grim, industrial,
made famous in his brother's *décimas*.
He put on a CD. "Listen to this."
At first I didn't recognize the voice
as rough and black as coal from under sea
shiny and ancient too with dreams of wood
and mined in sweat by men who would not bow.
"Roberto Parra.... he was always drunk
from boyhood on, just playing in the bars.
Uneducated, look at his writing.
A simple, noble soul. All that he earned
in Paris from *La Negra Ester*
he spent it all on whores...."
                        I asked to sing
and wondered who had touched that same guitar
(we never spoke of Violeta there)
a ballad of my father's life. He said:
"Your father was a year older than me.
I too knew Oxford, kind Port Meadow girls
for them a Chilean was most exotic.
My own father was distant. He died young.
That's why I never went for drink myself.
Come back tomorrow and we'll talk some more."

I joined the timid bathers in the waves
before breakfast, swam in that crimson sea
where they held one another fearfully.
I watched a diver working off the rocks
who gathered crabs and crawfish in a sack.
He was alone and unapproachable.
Then I returned to Nicanor again.
He said "Let's walk." It must have been round six.
He led the way along the coastal road.

And now it seemed to me that Parra looked
more like a Shaman than an Indian sage
an Inca Shaman, steely, focussed, wild,
regretting *la ferocidad perdida*
in poetry and in mankind as well.
The town came to an end in dirty sands
where we turned back. Women came up to him.
There was a funfair, people selling food.
A student and his girlfriend tore a box
of cigarettes for Nicanor to sign.
"My friend from England he's a poet too."
The next day was the one I had to leave.
The maid had been to San Antonio
to buy *marisco* - mussels which she steamed
and served us in a little dining room.
I asked if he would sign his book. He wrote
"for Christopher, *obispo de Londres,*
estas antiguallas del siglo XX"
(these antique lines of twentieth century verse).
We parted in the street - he held me close -
I said some words about 'an awkward bow.'
And now with tears and gladness in my heart
walked down the hill to board the waiting bus.

On the Way to Church I Noticed

Men with long brooms sweeping leaves from under cars
An Irishman on a bicycle with special mudguards
A fresh wild rotted orange tree stump
and a girl with orange hair framed in a white doorway
The smell of dead leaves and water which I call 'late Autumn'
Dzogchen Beara and the meditation room looking out over
   the misty sea
and three ships just discernible in the Cape Waters

A Ripple

A ripple on its journey to the grave
came riding through the room where silence held
sway - as in forests after trees are felled -
the air itself was like a water wave
where minnows flickered clouds of silver swelled

The Moorhen

Where the moorhen comes from no man knows
the egg or the horizon-
but still she ploughs
reeds bend even as the cold wind blows.

The Black Beetle

Utterly shiny goes the black beetle
over the sheep dung drying and grasses
the bracken divides the day like flames
and they bow to the jet black
                        machine as he passes.

Sonnet X

The sardine can I see so very clear
the flaky sardines in their golden oil
like corpses all dishevelled flaking foil
packed in as close as travellers so near
shoulder to shoulder on the underground
on fetid summer evenings turning home
no more like sharp adventurers to roam
in darksome waters where their friends are found
Their friendship now is tightness new defined
no breathing space, decapitated, tails
confined and sheltered finally in-sealed
and if to wiggle they were once inclined
now steep compression energy derails
until on opening day they are revealed.

The Old Woodland Yew

I come to the old woodland yew
when the frost is sprinkled like powder on the leaves
and the sun is a bright fiery seed.

He is in a quiet corner by the second pool
and I greet him with caution, respectfully,
by walking nine times around him.

He allows me to enter and rest in his fork.
His branches are extremely flexible.
His strength is pre-Industrial.

His roots are anchored deep
in leaf mould and the sandy soil
where foxes and young badgers in the spring

are watched by curious naturalists
who've rigged up lights among the trees.
I listened for a message:

The Yew asked me to come more often
and if I remembered the story of the fox
whose tail dangled in the well and froze -

I asked him his age:
He said four hundred years.
I left the yew walking in the direction of the sun
stumbling over foxholes.

The Taps

I wonder what kind of consciousness the taps have -
who cast their long grey shadows over the bathwater
making it darker
who await my coming at evening to turn them on or off
who are never sour or disgruntled
but gleam through the years of finger smears
shiny bold Centurions, one hot and one cold
sploshers providing me with what I need to get clean
as subtle influences on the earth as the planet Pluto

The Herons of Clonmel

Why doesn't God
give all the herons of Clonmel
as much fish as they want?

A slate-grey heron stands
at the far end of the long
man-made waterfall -
a ledge where branches and reflections are caught -
scratches its belly with its long neck
and pointed
fisherman's beak
while a white swan ducks
and a car goes past over the bridge.
St Mary's church is locked -
even the grounds are out of reach
behind gates
but the starlings are busy
in the tree tops -
Autumn - a spider has spun its thread -
from grassy fingers to coracled stone -
dead roots and violets -
a woman weighed down
with four polythene bags -
apparitions of warehouses -
with red shutters like army uniforms -
and a blue and white water storage box
rusty as a flag -
The heron is stiff and formal -
impregnates no maid
in this town
as your wild Uncle did.
Is attentive and can look in all directions -
The bridge juts into my stomach -
an octagonal sign says "STOP"
but I go on
admiring the river.

31st October, 1995, Clonmel, Ireland

Listening to Myself Singing

Listening to myself singing
in nineteen eighty
I can understand why they laughed
           (I laughed too)
and thought my Tragedy
was Comedy

It was like visiting hell
with your older self
or seeing a man
with a toothache, hearing his groans,
a man with a toothache,
made of stone, from an age before dentistry,
the wince, the slice, the blood of a scar....
the shouting like a voice
inside an incubator waiting to be born.

I Have Lived in Many Lonely Outposts

I have lived in many lonely outposts.
My coffin was carried up the long Blackwater valley.
On the night I was buried there was a terrible thunderstorm
and inappropriate dancing at Byblox House.
I have seen embroidery finer than lilies
and walked the city of Blake, Keats and Coleridge.

Today I Wear Magenta

Today I wear magenta.
My thumbs stick out at the back of me like chicken bones.
I am old and no longer go to parties.

Nothing here is stable.
Not even the trees in the puddles.

Coins of Summer

What have I got in my pocket?
some dust and gold and a piece of string
a coin with a tree on it
and one with the head of a king
a silver one with a sailing boat
because time pulls everybody under
but if you want real money
you've got to have coins of summer

There are seeds in the packet
put them in water and watch them grow
when she wakes from her long sleep
she gets up and goes to the window
tonight from Reigate we set sail
for shores of mystery and wonder
but you're not coming with me
unless you've got coins of summer

One with a tree without any leaves
one with a shirt with torn off sleeves
but you'll never know how
time bereaves
and pulls everybody under

Oh I like your jacket
blue silk and silver sleeves
they were walking in the landscape
kicking up the leaves
then one fine day she slipped away
from the eyes of her mother
better look in the graveyard
if you want to find coins of summer

She was close to her father
and me I never saw
in the old dispensation
before you came on board
when music hung from every bough
and poets did surround her
I could make my offering now
but I've only got coins of summer

The Cuckoos

Well the old love cheats
who live down by the bushes
where the streams run by
and the white water gushes
Hear the song of the branches
and reflections in the weir
the cuckoos are back
in the valley this year

Florence Nightingale's ghost
does the hospital rounds
Wheelchairs and perambulators
abandoned in the grounds
An army of wounded
walk slowly to the West
for them winter came early
to the cuckoo's nest

Yodelay hey hey yodeleedle odelay hey
Yodelay hey hey yodeleedle odelay hey

Planets are shaking
like an ashtray in spring
Fag ends are falling
on the Head of Christ the King
And the old love cheats
how they whisper in my ear
the cuckoos are back
in the valley this year

Yodelay hey hey yodeleedle odelay hey
Yodelay hey hey yodeleedle odelay hey

Donkey Composition

Donkeys' heads like old boots
in the blackened doorway
and straw and mud and eyes like wounds
or nostrils or mouths
grey-brown as sand
tidal refuse
with goat beards
looking out at me
indifferent -
March rains, damp earth -
cars grate and shudder
and strain and whoosh
Big Pipe lorries sent by God
most curiously
I am learning your language of signs -
puns and confusion -
Pipes with big rounded ends
wrapped in cerulean blue plastic -
from the Little Pipe
to the Wide Estuary -
the donkeys' ears are handlebars
I hold them and ride
backwards into Infinity.

The Conception

It was a night of cold
clear and starry weather
when the man and the woman
lay in bed together

Leaves were rustling
along the drive in the dawn
and a fox ran
across the lawn

The woman rolled over
the man fell asleep
and I swam inland
where the cliffs are steep

And the snow was light
and the snow was cold
and the house was warm
and the husband was bold

It snowed on the hills
up by the four stones
and it snowed on the buried
Rector's bones

And the woman's love
flowed warm and sweet
from her fingertips
to the soles of her feet

And the snow was light
and the snow was cold
and the house was warm
and the lovers were bold

All the windows lit up
and the bells did chime
when you came across
from the other side of time

Above Glasbury

When the river came round the bend at Llyswen
The waves were in steps like the sea
It was foaming and muddy and passionate then
and seemed to go on ceaselessly

John Twigg

Born in Handsworth, Birmingham
in 1913
First thing he remembered
was the flight of a zeppelin
His little brother died
who could have been his friend
Now he's running home from school
afraid the world might end

St John's College Oxford
he never learned to dance
but he loved to climb the mountains
of Switzerland and France
Here they are outside the refuge
starting out at dawn
with sunglasses and wooly hats
to climb the Matterhorn

War came, he'd joined the Church
He wasn't called to fight
He was the Bishop's Chaplain
(I hope I've got this right)
He went to live in Somerset
where times were not so hard
First a Curate in Wolverhampton
and then the Vicar of Chard

He married many couples
He'd celebrate Saints' Days
He liked to talk to people
who were puzzled by God's ways
He preached about the Sower
and the Sermon on the Mount
He said the Rise and Fall of a Sparrow
was a matter of great account

Here he is in a dark suit
crouching by the sea
and the little boy with the wooden spade
in the photograph is me
He seems to look beyond us
out into the waves
Sometimes I'm making sandcastles
and then it's drowned mens' graves

The last one that we had of him
was taken by the thieves
He was laughing with my mother
and his hand was on her knee
He was dying and he knew it
but he didn't look afraid
I just wish that he could have told me
all those things he never said

Rimbaud's Grave

There was snow as I got off the train
the train that had come from Paris via Rheims
snow along the platform, frosty air,
men in boots - it could have been Russia -
the East certainly -
Charleville-Mézières-
I'd been there in dreams....
I stayed in a hotel with high ceilings
and a view out over the snowy square.
I saw the house where Rimbaud had lived for a time
and visited the museum
I think I saw the poet's old brown suitcase
returned from Africa
and a poster of Rimbaud in jeans
like a prototype beat poet, prototype backpacker -

I never found the cemetery
instead I sacrificed a chicken
(already dead) and tore its carcass
to pieces in the street, tearing off
strips of flesh to eat - it was good
hot and cooling, garlicky - a troop
of schoolboys came up the hill
as I was going down
and I scattered the bones in the snow
of that detestable town.

The Poet Speaks of Mobile Phones

I
Foul little plastic implement of deafness and dissociation
strangler
with invisible cheesewires
screwing the air into little balls
fucker up of ley lines
your bleep is the end of poetry
your buzz is worse than the bite of a dinosaur
pterodactyl get out of my railway carriage
Mobile phone you don't know which way is north or south
your mouth full of rotten teeth smells of ten day old oranges
you are destroying my arteries
Weeper of toxicity
Starver of light to underwater plants
When will you split in half?
How many heads have you?
You cannot migrate or take part in any rituals
and yet you outnumber the stars in the Milky Way
I was given one once I used it as a trowel
It took two thousand years to disintegrate
I open your lid
and find your head full of maggots
wriggling like the contents of a fisherman's box
You carry on after car crashes

II
Angels have been getting tangled in your invisible dragnets
Unfriendly to dolphins you have de-horned the moon
In Wales your masts take up the choicest hilltops
while dead sheep and lambs rot in the farmyards
too heavy to bury -
you separate the head from the body
To use you once is equivalent to a bad LSD trip
The sparrows are departed
leaving no addresses
millions of vodaphones have come in their place -
They loiter evilly by the drinking fountains
Unloveable dildoes
Wands incapable of transformations!
You violate the integrity of spaces!
Along with your brother the television
you have destroyed my imagination
made natural telepathy a blessing not for our lifetimes
Children should not know of you
and the time of your existence be perceived
as a shameful period on earth.

A View in Gloucester

Pink posters curling at the top
stuck on glass
with special jellied suckers
Gifts for Mum in dark blue
                (almost black)
                        letters.
Two pairs of slippers.
One with flowers
One showing ducklings
                cuddling.
Seagulls above squabbling,
islands of gum on the pavement
crab shells, fag ends, manholes, squares
of concrete - and the cardboard boxes stacked
awkwardly like hay bales not as
                well as hay bales
pale brown, light brown, dark brown
with masking tape wrinkled and crinkled
and words SHOE ZONE
                CUST ORDER
                and FELIXSTOWE
imported, customer order six
made in China
safe in Gloucester
Gifts for Mum, Two ninety nine
why pay more?
Subject to availability
They look soft and wooly
from here, they look smooth and padded
they look like home for suppurating feet
for the whole disaster that is the human.

Self Portrait

I am Christopher Twigg, the ape, the sycophant,
    the hypochondriac,
the recycler of bottles and stern self critic,
the lover and hater of poetry,
the closet atheist, the believer in countless world
    religions,
the Bombay charlatan with ominous vials of red liquid.

I am Christopher Twigg, the thief,
the supporter of charities;
the wader of turquoise oceans,
and fashionable shopper at Safeways.
(My basket is loaded with razor shells and tinned asparagus.)

I am Christopher Twigg, the generous host of parties,
the provoker of orgies,
the genteel *Bed and Breakfast* landlady,
the Parisian taxi driver,
the scribbling drunk - it was me you saw
in the station bar at Ostend -
the patient waiter for my own soul to catch up with me.

I am Christopher Twigg, the painter of twee landscapes and
    sentimental nudes,
the artist whose work is easy
and impossible to understand,
the poet in three languages,
the inexperienced lecturer, the unfulfilled academic and pedant:
that converted barn of a man.

I am Christopher Twigg, the imperialist,
the starter of wars and vertical invader of other planets,
the anonymous, abusive telephone caller,
a friend to the blind and the elderly,
compassionate before real life and the television.

My Heart is like a Stony Mountainside

My heart is like a stony mountainside
dry in the sun where donkeys' hoofs dislodge
the tumbling rocks which scatter fall and slide
above them is the path where heroes trudge
in leather hats with bundles and with flags
some smoke, some drink, some laugh and jangle coins
and ever higher climb among these crags
and ever on that slope the hard sun shines
My heart is like a bathtub dusty dry
the taps are disconnected there's no plug
only the odd insect came there to die
purple and orange plums are on the jug
the one I used to use to wash my hair
in kinder days when there was water there.

Winded by Drinking

Winded by drinking
but still wanting more
I remember you at parties
at 45 degrees
like somebody's
twenty-two year old grandmother
swaying blissfully
as you filled up your lungs.

Highgate Pond

A pool of living water on the heath
when golden autumn shines and floods the trees
The pike lie on the bottom underneath
a wall of leaves that no one ever sees
The year is suffering its hero's death
I venture out along the diving boards
Then seal like I surface and draw breath
and gasp with cold it cuts my legs like swords
Crossing the water, stinging, burning womb
my fingers and my toes begin to numb
Dilapidated spacious rooms of gloom
where feet and limbs of wood together come
and irritation fades away like mud
and I'm awake the tree is in my blood

Brittany Ferries

Spring finds me on the car deck
where I lie like a cigarette end
relishing my freedom.
Behind me a Spanish school party
study the constellations.

My bunk has pink sheets
and a ladder to reach it.
A corduroy crimson sofa,
a shower and a basin
with threads of vomit that the cleaners missed.

I visit *Captain Colin's Magic Show*
for boys and girls under seven
full of innuendo
he has wands that droop and mysteriously erect themselves,
balloons with teats,
a handkerchief that gathers like a tentpole.

I stand among the grown-ups beyond glass
in the *Yacht Club* bar. The setting sun
is an egg yolk
softly added to the sea's cocktail.
A boy they've dressed as Tarzan flexes his muscles
the rising moon has water on the brain
hydrocephalic -
It staggers naked like a zombie
through the streets of Milwaukee.

Here in this floating hospital
with *Chanel* and *Fabergé* counters,
I request songs from the pianist, wintering
I can't remember anything.
My name is Christopher. My tooth mug came
wrapped in plastic. The bedpan is stained
as if it had been fried
too long by accident.
The Captain has asked me
to turn my lights out at night
so he can navigate.
Spray and woodland then ice
and bare rock.
On the third morning I wake
to snow on the roofs of the lorries.

The Hungry Ghost in Paris

Flashlights go off like hydrogen bombs
inside the cathedral of Notre Dame.
Discreetly unhappy I sweat in my trousers;

my waistcoat is furred with cigarette ash.
My weariness is one leaf,
one oak leaf; my stream of piss

hits an empty water bottle
under a car.
I grimace

at two girls
fingering dry chips
in McDonalds.

In a shower without soap
or adequate towelling
I dry myself on extended grey-white sheets.

The two Marys
confront themselves
in mirrors.

The water at my feet
is gritty, puddingy
where oily snakes have disassembled.

Outside in the street
men go to work - early morning,
Islamic, real rain -

My candle gutters
on a heap of candles
in Notre Dame.

Embers

Embers are capsules of heat
in the dark, on the ground
Glowing red as insects' eggs
defying the darkness around
Ever fading containers
of heat of warmth as I said
a small city of fires and lights
where the sandalled foot may tread
With a charred and glowing pointed stick
I scrape the embers away
scattering them with earth, folding them under
till their glows extinguish; there are a few stars
in the vast and empty sky, cold night
the owl flies across to the blasted tree
and the current of the river flows merrily.

A Priest

Fat bloated kindly face
Swelling cheeks like sacks of wheat
milky and deaf -
man of equivalents
short-haired with eyes far back
Jaw stern and firm
eyes cheated and defeated
a boxer who will not give up
who gave himself up long ago-
whose intentions are stars
which guide him to nest
            and harbour-

They Didn't Think the Truth Mattered

They didn't think the Truth mattered
   so any words would do
The enemies I could have scattered
   I was forbidden to

A Tasmanian

I couldn't see where he had come in from
but when I looked up he was there
with a red medieval balaclava on.

"Is today Sunday? Then it will have to be
a Day of Rest" he said in an accent I thought Scottish.
"Is there a launderette in town, a café anywhere?"

The church bell tolled, light rain.
"I need to find where the track begins, tomorrow's
track..." I asked him where he lived.

"Tasmania. Last night I slept in a field
of uncut grass... two pounds the Publican charged me.
The river could rise. I've seen hikers in New Zealand

lose everything in a sudden flood. Now I must find the track."
With that he turned and walked away from us.

For Keith Gems

A clearance in the mist, unearthly scenes
of sea-bird crowded waters, singing caves;
the backs of basking sharks like submarines,
a prehistoric fin that cuts the waves.
That stillness when the engine is turned off:
the wash and swell, the lap and kiss of foam....
two figures in the dark, a snore, a cough....
I sleep on deck, in rain and moon, at home.
We race up to Glengarriff. *Passim* moored
by wooded islands, swimming seal and dog....
He rows through peaty water, climbs on board,
relaxes, lights the oil lamp, writes the log.
A Man who somehow knows he has been Blessed
and wants to share his Blessing with the Rest.

The Old Balladeer

It happened in Hammersmith
one bloody day
An old Balladeer
came singing away
With his pram and his bucket
He cried "welladay
Have a Song from an old Balladeer"

The people they saw him
they shouted abuse
They kicked in his pram
and they stole all his juice
His face which was beetroot
well now it was puce
Oh alas for a poor balladeer

They twisted his arms off
and damaged his balls
They poked at his nipples
It was serious assault
They plucked out his windpipe
and they put it in salt
and said "Sing on you old Balladeer"

He said "I never did mean
to upset anyone"
They said "fuck you you arsehole
you nose full of scum
You've offended our Queen
and offended her Son
now be silent you old Balladeer"

Well the Balladeer rose
from his wounds and despair
and he reached for his windpipe
and put it back where
a windpipe belongs
and he drew in fresh air
and said "still I'm an old Balladeer"

But they did in the old Balladeer
the way I'd predicted they would
by Hammersmith bridge
he was sunk in a fridge
through air and through water to mud
and the headlights of cars did not notice
no torches were shone on the crime
where the Balladeer drowned now a boat is
and the river keeps watch of his time

The Ballad of the Shropshire Lorry

Three walkers on a Norfolk road
one dark October night
When a brightly lit-up lorry showed
It was a wondrous sight

Like the fairy lights on a Christmas tree
advancing quiet and slow
As we leaned back into the hedge
They wound down the window

I said "Quick, let's play the tambourines
and beat out strange percussion"
There were three men in the steamed-up cab
They could have been Turkish or Russian

"We're not sure if we're on the right road"
All three men did laugh
"We've come across country from Shropshire
and we're strangers in these parts

And someone told us there's a pub
at the bottom of this lane
And whatever you've been drinking
We would like the same"

Then James he struck the little drum
I shook my tambourine
They gave six blasts upon their horn
and vanished like a dream

When we got back to the warm fireside
and the friends we used to know
We told them about this story
that happened so long ago

On Madness

A man looks over on his life and all he sees is ash.
He goes to the fire and stirs it up -
or where there was a fire.
It's all ash today.
So he stirs the charred remains,
Finds some charcoal,
Some embers which still glow orange
like a sun set
but he looks around
and pauses and then says
It's all ash today.
The people I loved
The ones I hardly knew
Love I don't know what it was
Only the sea is blue
Where the waves and seagulls play.
It's all ash today.

Bathtime in the Country

It's bathtime in the country
and the snow is lying deep
It's bathtime in the country
and the lanes are full of sheep
It's bathtime in the country
and the carts are in the pond
It's bathtime in the country
and we're sailing on and on

It's bathtime in the country
and the cars are in the hills
It's time to go to school again
and pay your heating bills
It's bathtime in the country
Are there blessings for the meek?
It's bathtime in the country
and we're falling fast asleep

Oh and I know that
because I go there
Yes and I know that
because I go there

It's bathtime in the country
and my head is stuck with leaves
The harvest has all been and gone
and they're binding up the sheaves
It's bathtime in the country
and my heart is heavy lead
It's bathtime in the country
and I'm singing in my bed

Yes and I know that
because I go there
Oh and I know that
because I go there

Goldfish Memory

Goldfish swim
with their memories round them
and that is where
in the ice I found them
like autumn leaves
all golden red
and like the leaves
these fish were dead

I saw the man
walk through the pasture
with a heavy stick
and my heart beat faster
but the goldfish hearts
or whatever they were
had stopped like clocks
at the beginning of the year

The trains ran on
and the buildings rose
and the winter was hard
and the pipes all froze
and the builders came
with their old stepladders
and the grandparents crossed
to the land of shadows

Astley Woods

I was afraid to go into the wood last night
on the way back from Astley, from the church
with the Elizabethan effigies, to Glasshampton.
I had been in the wood on my way there, the wood was alright
then, it was still light, but becoming spooky
a tree stump with shoots for a second I took for a crowned head -
birds were disturbed, fluttering - badgers
had not yet started their running -
there was a stream of water, there were many leaves
and the path could have been easy to lose
so I turned home by a long and inconvenient way
through a field of lettuces past a farm
with a fishing pool and signs and gates which clanged
as I passed guiltily and thrilled the way to the road

My Sacred Grass with Leaves Set in it

My sacred grass with leaves set in it
and wind sighing over it
        at twilight on a rainy day
Red traffic lights burn
A white polythene bag rides among the twigs
Leaves wobble and shelter
like old suitcases,
        eco-friendly shrouds
sails gone awry
drops of rain on the blades like tickertape
purplish earth showing through dungy
like the hair of an old green dog
        shaggy with melancholy
shaking its back incommunicado by a pond

I Like the Jesus Army

I like the Jesus army.
I wanted to go on their bus.
Their chanting is more like Hindoos than Christians.
They play guitars and jump up and down like biologists.

Everyone can see the Jesus army are genuinely happy -

Even to fundamentalists I extend the hand of friendship.

Squirrels

Squirrels hang
upside down under sycamore branches
like tadpoles
They came here on UFOs.
They work in pairs
and smell eachother's arseholes.
They are not afraid of Death
but when the tree has gone they are empty
the Ivy has climbed higher
than any body knows.

A Puritan

The lady opposite has turquoise socks
that almost match
the top of her thermos flask which makes a cup
from which she drinks hot coffee.
I wish well to the lady
and hope she enjoys her coffee.
But I must say -
I do not like the ways she eats her sandwiches -
brown crusts which she protectively cradles in her fists.
She thinks she is abstemious;
I think she is a puritan.

The Altar-Pisser

An altar-pisser came to Belbroughton Church
and pissed on or behind the altar
Some say he pissed in the vestry as well
Others that he slept all night in the porch by candlelight
that he splashed cider at the foot of the old Yew
and drank Newcastle Brown Ale by the lych-gate
Some that he tried to climb the tower
He was sub-normal, backward, odd or angry,
in need of help certainly,
lonely, outcast,
with a dark stream between his legs
that one day bled.

On Gurnard's Head

I
Would that you were here with your flute, Antonio,
for these days of light and rain.
We would improvise songs about Nature
like hens who seek out seeds in the wet grass.

All day I've played on Gurnards Head -
a granite tent God pitched against the sea -
calling myself 'devout'
and 'secretary of Nature'.

The scrape and boom among the rocks.
A coalman delivering sacks
to a Rectory cellar.
Slabs big as dining room tables
glow golden-green under the water.

Bedraggled porpoise-stomached shags
flap their wings like umbrellas.

A seal noses through the undergrowth
with glistening belly
spotted like an aquatic thrush.

And then at three o'clock the dolphins passed -
a holy sight -
granting me glimpses of their backs and fins.

II
The sea has no addresses. Only roads
which fluctuate and change from day to day.
The housemartins and bumble bees of Treen
sing in seven dimensions.

Under the apple tree
there you became my betrothed
There I gave you my hand
and you were healed
in the same place where your mother was taken

The cows came by with heavy udders
like bursting sacks of grain
dribbling silver threads at the nostrils
and holding up the cars.

Now the Bride has entered
into the lush and long desired meadow
Now she rests at ease in its atmosphere
her neck reclined
on the soft arms of her Beloved

I watch the foxglove's purple sway.
The bald head of the sea glitters.

These Coastal Taxi Drivers who I Meet at Night

These coastal taxi drivers who I meet at night
after a long day's walking
I pay a fare - equivalent
to a hotel room, nearly -
and they take me home -
I rainswept -
they in a world of car radios and cigarettes -

They always did some other job before
in some wild metropolis like Brussels
or London - but here they are
in Bostraeth, Gwennap or the end of the world
Porthgwarra some quiet
corner in England -
with no local bus

In Praise of a Friend I Met in the Street

It was not his shirt or his health or his eyes I noticed
but the warm feeling in my heart
rising from my navel like summer shrubbery.

Samhain

The year is gaining on the hour
The hour is rubbing out the year
beneath the faded pencil marks
the old ancestral lines appear

All Saints' Day, Kilmallock

An oxygen lorry succeeds
an egg lorry
through the Blossom Gate
at Kilmallock.
Outside there is mist; inside
a town asleep.
'They won't be about for
a little while now'
said the man who had slept
all night in front of the television
His Guinness had been left -

The stern unknowable face
of the man on the Turin shroud
looked down from among
the family photographs
in the dusty breakfast room where I slipped
ten pounds under a tea cup -

So I came to the Blossom Gate,
one of five,
the last survivor
Gone were John's (West),
Friar's (North), Water Gate
and Ivy Gate on the East side -
(In those days were towns
meant for happiness?)
Arrow slits and nasturtiums -
Shaggy ink caps in the wet grass of the long field
and the burned Dominican Priory -
The flight of jackdaws like shaking out a duvet -

Listening to My Mother

I get moved
listening to my mother -
sitting outside
in the garden at Hinchley Cottage -
in folding summer chairs -
and she remembers
how she loved
summer evenings as a girl
when she was in bed and heard
her parents' voices in the garden -
"I just used to love hearing them" she says
and I am moved and try not to show it
and she is moved and shows it a little -
"they'd have gone out after supper" –
"What would they be doing?" I ask.
"Oh, they'd be looking at things" -
the purple irises among the high green grass
by the plastic bag with the compost -
the Needham's orchard beyond -
a spotted flycatcher nesting precariously
upon the garage rafter -
things I only started to notice properly
since I was ill -
that golden thread which as Machado says
links memories to soul -
I rejoice in the tears and the sorrow
for I know my life is real -
my losses are real, my body is real,
my hymns and hands are real -
I feel their passing wisdom -
the voices of my dead
grandparents in the garden.

Melon Sermon

To Sun readers they mean breasts
but not to me.
Melons are melons.
Made of water and pulp like us and the planet.

Their juice is good enough to drive a car on
Their yellow skin I've seen mapped out with roads

Was there ever a poet
who sang exclusively of melons?
Who praised their slush and slime
the run of their pips?
Who decorated his house yellow in homage to them?

Their juice is good enough to drive a car on

If you plant melon seeds
you don't get melons
you get lanterns.
Are not twenty worth a glass of tea?
After eating fifty I begin to hallucinate.
Then the bazaar becomes
a frightening place.
"This isn't Europe now" the melons seem to be saying
"you cannot go here without a guide."
And they keep reappearing
round steps and from behind fountains.

Their yellow skin I've seen mapped out with roads

Melons, models of sobriety, we use them
to ornament churches.
One day I ate so many I lost consciousness.
When I came to
I was in a field of yellow birds
like seagulls at harvest festival time.

Their juice is good enough to drive a car on
Their yellow skin I've seen mapped out with roads

The River at Kington

Dusty mercurial moonlight dull as zinc
shivered on the rippling surface of the Arrow

the river Arrow running over stones
broken glass and broken pottery

scissors for animal surgery, a green fire extinguisher.
The moon in the alders high on clarity

the boggy grass, the mud slide, the flood
where tomorrow I stood

disentangling barbed wire and clearing the grid
of sticks and brown bottles and autumn foam...

the moonlight so gentle and otherworldly
here in the present and in no hurry

to be gone, like St Peter, in an act of Charity
relieving with its silver earthly poverty.

Poem in Spanish

Yo soy el obispo de Londres
y desayuno con musli, yogur y té
y me visto con una camisa blanca;
escribo en mi habitación
con la ventana muy abierta.

Yo soy el obispo de Londres.
Y me acuerdo de mi amiga, Daniela,
con quién lo pasaba muy bien
en la ciudad de Frankfurt.

Tengo sueños eróticos, necesidades
inmensos como la mar

porque yo soy el obispo de Londres.

Escucho las lágrimas
que bajan las escaleras de tu casa;
las mismas que subo yo
mi deseo luchando con mi vergüenza.

Sí que soy el obispo de Londres!

Oigo el viento que sopla
como un aliento verde en las copas de los árboles
y pienso aún en la cicatriz
de mi compañera, Daniela.

Bananas Make a Good Breakfast

I
Bananas make a good breakfast.
Two white sustaining horns
newly undressed
with traces of fibre still clinging
to their blanched softnesses.
Rough dry outsides, smooth wet in-
-side flesh.
Yields easily to the knife.
No need to eat them lewdly but you can.
Their yellow skin:
no jaundice ever went that far.
One banana
can feed a tribe of ants
for ten years.
A fly
eats twice its weight in bananas
in a day.
I stick a drawing pin
in the side of the banana
(in search of yellow blood).
I inject the banana
with sulphuric acid
(to make it orange).
I leave boot-prints in the banana.
I hang one up outside a fish shop
and call it 'the yellow Christ'.
I press one on the strings of my guitar.
It falls into seven pieces.

II
Bananas compared with cucumbers

Greenness does not indicate a cucumber is not ripe.
Their flesh is translucent whereas
that of the banana is opaque.
Banana: blotting paper, cloudy water.
You can wait years for a banana to clear - it never will -
People have been reading the newspaper
through cucumbers for generations.
Neither are much good for printing,
but the banana leaves a blurred impression.
Its juice is mucous
not watery like the cucumber's.
We could say
the banana has a worse cold than the cucumber.

The Snails of Boswednack

I make high-pitched sounds
to disturb
the snails of Boswednack....
Two of them, courting,
in their yellow shells,
a dumb yellow that shines
with slime....
Two snails on a dead branch
of bracken, orange-brown,
in the new green grass....
Maytime....   the snails are coupling
unaware
of pollution, the threat
to the ozone layer
and other good reasons
for not having children....
The snails explore each other's mouths,
eking out nuance of gender and age,
details....   are they blind? Have they
the most exquisite smells?
On their rafter or raft
there in the fresh green grass
by the well-trodden path, the newly paved road
ascending from the white house
where the two red cars are parked....
by the purple bluebells and the slate-grey sea....
where seagulls wheel
and threaten the traveler,
the yellow snails
with their long horns
which expand and protrude,
rough like slugs on the outside....
rubber suckers sticky
of the eternal female
snail
The horns like pins of flesh
with pin heads
and mouths which pulsate
and reach across

to a mate
on a dead bracken branch
there in the long fresh green grass,
where the newly paved road goes down
to where the two red cars are parked.

The Song of my Conception

At my Conception I sang
with the Voice of Snow
quiet and numbing pain
I lay along branches and gravestones
No finger passed through me

I sang as a blanket beneath the clear stars
I was a peasant beneath the golden vault
and lay with a white-boned boy
in horse hair and coughing -

I was a draught and the fire burned up
fruiting flames into the blackened chimney

Keep me grounded Keep me safe
I sang with the dry oak leaves
and the singing was neither from within or without
neither from chimney or from sky
but from the memory of bone

I sang in the lit-up windows
of the nineteenth-century church
and my voice was a wet sob
staining the carpet -
I sang in the subdued blood of my Father
and in the breasts of my mother -

My voice stirred among centuries-old leaves
and red mulch
branches and bracken and fox fur

and the bells of the Seventeenth Century responded
to my song
and I was the snow
and the bird's footprints in the snow
and the first greedy blue-tit
at the newly delivered milk bottle
pecking through tin foil -

Our Father

Our Father who art in heaven
Weighed down by every kind of problem
With a frown like our foreign secretary
or a vulgar ordinary man
You don't have to worry about us any more.

We understand that you are suffering
That you can't get matters organized
We know the Devil won't leave you in peace
How he deconstructs everything that you build.

He makes fun of you
but we don't. We cry with you.
Don't be upset by his diabolical laughter.

Our Father who art where thou art
surrounded by disloyal angels
Sincerely: Don't go on suffering on our account.
Try to come to terms with it:
Gods are not infallible
and we can forgive everything.

Translated from 'Padre Nuestro' by Nicanor Parra

Joe Strummer and the Art Student

I'm in the French House with a picture book.
I am aware that Joe is in the room.
I thought though he was drinking at the bar.
When I look up he's standing at my table.
The hero of my twenties. His voice to me
so full of love and pity for the world.
He'd thought that he was Jesus once, on drugs,
but knew he wasn't good or clean enough.

The River Usk at Newport, brown and dull,
the bedroom with guitars and typewriter
the comic strips, the girlfriends up from London,
the private sweetness of this Gentleman
all come into my mind when he is there,
his voice, one said, like rust under a car
the voice of one defeated and yet just
who cried "Don't push us" at the uniforms.

He asks me who I am and what I do
and I reply with confused awkwardness:
"I am an Art Student." (What shall I say?)
"I went to Art School too, but not for long.
Some day I'd like to see some of your work...."
He slunk off back to join his drinking friends.
His heart gave out at fifty. I had dreamed
one time he'd hear my songs this friend who sang
of fields of wheat, a rose worth living for.

To Rafael Gutiérrez Quesada

You taught me to eat whole bulbs of garlic for lunch
with cheese, bread and red wine to wash them down.
We chewed white teeth between our teeth
on week long walks in the Sierra Nevada.
You taught me how it's OK to get drunk at high altitudes
provided the wine is pure and 'without chemicals'.
That way you just have a good sleep
and wake without a hangover.
We bought *litres and litres* from Pedro in Trevélez
and carried them arduously up the donkey paths
with Walt Whitman
and *the hundred best poems in the Spanish language*.
You said "The Odyssey's a marvellous book"
and hated the moon when she was full:
on those nights you would not drink from mountain streams
for fear of tasting blood.
We slept in caves, in shepherds' huts and on threshing floors,
we lay in riverbeds surrounded by leeches,
smoked *Celtas* and imagined we were hiding from Franco.
You made tea from Alpine flowers.
At Siete Lagunas we crossed the snowbound meadow with bare
                                                        feet.
Climbing summits you showed me how to feel each step
and think less of getting to the top.
And then you came to England.
You saw dwarves in the plane trees above the King's Road
and would not walk up Dark Lane in the dark.
Your cigarettes smelt of burning car tyres.
You were so drunk you were incontinent
and left a wet patch in my mother's armchair.
My bourgeois pride was hurt. You wanted to drink the brandy
we were keeping for the Christmas pudding!
I left you at the airport early.

Gutiérrez Quesada, the same surname as Don Quijote . . .
the last I heard of you you were a waiter,
serving breakfast to English tourists in Palma de Mallorca.

Santiago

A city seen as jewels in the night
was Santiago as my plane flew north
I'd sobered down my head it wasn't right
the seas of darkness had engulfed the earth
and all was settled blue black like a map
Aladdin's chest was scattered on the cloak
so infinite the wealth in fortune's lap
the love that hadn't happened turned to smoke
and there it was the city on display
with strings of pearls and ornaments that shine
she looked down....   as if she'd say....
and then she smiled, said "all this can be mine"
and gathered in the treasure in her arms
not I alone was taken with her charms

To the Round Moon

Round moon you come to my window
like a pregnant belly or a searchlight
to verify my activities,
to check all's well
with my television licence and my neighbours.
You are as detached and efficient as a therapist
or McDonalds employee.
You wear a white coat like a surgeon
and clear the dead wasps from my drawers.

Welcome moon to shine in on my house and life.
All's pure in here you'll find.
No filthy poppies do enseam
my moon bed, my moon armchair,
my moon boots with the compass hidden in the heel.
All's *lunar* here you'll find.

Oh moon, dogfish cold and unshaven
I saw you loaded into vans at Finisterre.
By your light the French camera crew video the Kaffir dancers,
the heroin is smuggled successfully into Dover,
the seaweed reaches the surface at double its usual rate.
I call upon you now
to bless my friend Adam
and guide him safe to Compostela.

Christopher Twigg was born in 1958 and studied at Pembroke College, Cambridge (English Literature) and the Slade School of Art (Painting). He taught English in Comprehensive schools in south and west London and then moved to Granada, Andalusia, where he learned Spanish and began to draw and paint. He noticed a change in his writing in 1991 and published his first collection, Adventures in the West, in 1993. This was followed by In the Choir in 1997 (Alces Press), which was "Paperback of the Week" in the Guardian newspaper. He is a founding member of the alternative country group Chicken of the Woods and now lives in Wales.